HOW TO BE A STAND-UP COMIC IN 21 DAYS

That funny Gal!

ISBN: 978-81-69067-87-4 (Paperback)

Author: That Funny Gal
Published by: The Crackajack Company

First Edition: 2026

Before We Begin

Read them.

Or waste three weeks.

The Final Truth

(that no one wants to hear)

What Comes Next

(If you're actually doing this)

You are Already That Person.

Start Talking.

Bonus Materials & Resources

P.S. The audience is not smarter than you. They are just listening harder.

P.P.S. The first time you bomb, it will feel catastrophic. It isn't.

P.P.P.S. If you never bomb, you are not pushing far enough.

P.P.P.P.S…

You are warned. No refunds; enter at your own risk

The 21-Day Comedy Workbook

Train Your Brain to Think in Jokes (Without Trying Too Hard)

Before We Begin: The Fine Print.

This Isn't a "Find Your Funny" Workshop.

You are Already Observing the World Sideways—You Just Keep Apologising For it.

This Workbook Is About Noticing What You are Already Doing When No One's Grading You.

Chill. Have Fun.
You Got This!

The Non-Negotiables:

Write Daily. Bad Writing Counts. Especially Bad Writing.

Your Worst Sentences Are Doing Reconnaissance Work—

They Re Showing You What Not to Say, Which Is 80% of Comedy.

Speak Jokes Out Loud. Comedy Lives in Air, Not Paper.

A Joke on 'the Page Is a Recipe. A Joke Spoken Is a Meal. You Can't Taste a Recipe.

Abandon 'Tm Not Funny" Thoughts Immediately. That's Just Fear Doing Admin Work.

Fear Loves Paperwork: Filing Complaints, Organizing Evidence, Building Cases Against Joy. Don't Let It.

15-25 Minutes Per Day, Maximum.

Consistency Beats Brilliance. Always.

You Are Not Trying to Write a Special. You are Trying to Rewire How You Notice 'Things.

No Performing for ‘the Workbook. This Is Practice, Not Audition.

Write Like Someone Who Does Not Need to Impress the Paper.

Week One:

Excavation

(finding what you already know)

Day 1

Your Comedy Origin Story

this is not about your first joke. It is about you first noticing your thoughts and your voice.

Write freely for 15 minutes.

a) When did you first realize you observe people differently?

(Hint: probably childhood. Probably when you got in trouble for it.)

b) What makes people laugh when you're not trying to be funny—when you're annoyed, confused, or just explaining something?

c)What do you notice that others walk past?

Patterns? Hypocrisies?

The gap between what people say and what they actually do? Now read what you wrote.

Circle one sentence that sounds exactly like you—not the you who' trying to sound smart, but the you who texts friends at 2 a.m. That sentence is your raw voice. It's unpolished. It probably has a typo. Protect it.

Day 2

What Annoys You (the Actual Gold Mine)

Forget what makes you laugh.

Start with what makes you cringe. Like

a) People who say "I'm just being honest" right before they stab you with words and expect you to thank them for the knife

b) LinkedIn hustle porn about waking up at 4am to conquer the day (bro, you sell marketing software, you're not saving the world from war, or death or earthquakes or... you get the point)

c) "Let's circle back" (translation: "I will actively avoid you until you forget this conversation happened")

d) Adults who call themselves "foodies" (you're not a foodie, you just have a credit card and don't care about your health or appearance)

e) Therapy-speak weaponized: "I need to protect my peace" = 'I'm allowed to be terribly rude to you now; my Shrink gave me the permission to do that"

f) People who say they're bad with technology, gazing into that iPhone they fully customized.

g) "Living my best life" posted as a candid, no filter selfie that somehow took you 47 clicks to get right. I was there! Stop lying!

h) Couples who refer to themselves as "we" as if they are the same person and in third person. "We don't eat gluten"
So you couldn't tell me that when before I invited you for a pasta and poker evening?"

i) "I'm an empath."

Said exclusively by people who've made you feel like shit and then blamed you for their shit.

j) Anyone who says "Normalize" "Normalize crying."

We are. Disney drops a tear-jerker every six months.

k) Motivational quotes over sunsets posted by people who have just woken up from their hangover.

I) “Sorry not sorry.” Pick a lane dude. Commit. That is what grownups do.

Pick one thing. Finish this sentence:
“The weird thing about ___ is...”

No jokes yet. Just truth.

Write three sentences about why it bothers you. Not the surface reason. The real reason.

Example:

The weird thing about "I'm just being honest". It's never about honesty. It's about permission. They're asking you to sit still while they wound you, then thank them for their bravery.

Why this matters:

Irritation is clarity with adrenaline. It means you see something clearly that others have normalized. That clear-seeing, not the anger itself, is the joke.

Warning sign:

If your list is 10 versions of "people are stupid," go deeper. That's lazy. Specificity is where comedy lives.

Day 3

Opinions You Hide

Write 5 opinions you are too polite to say in public. The ones you edit mid-sentence.

The ones you'd say to one friend but not at a dinner party.

Examples:
"I don't hate self-care. I just hate how it makes me feel about my lack of self-care"

"Minimalism is just rich people discovering what poor people already know."

"I don't trust people whose entire personality is their mental health diagnosis."

"Vulnerability is a currency now, and everyone's inflating it."

"Being 'authentic' has become another performance. We're exhausted in new ways."

Now do this:

Underline the most uncomfortable one.

That discomfort? That's comedy knocking.

It's afraid you won't answer.

Add one line:
"The part I can't say out loud is..."

Finish that sentence.

Write what comes after when no one's listening.

Why this matters:

The opinions you hide haven't been focus grouped into mush.

They still have teeth.

Comedy needs teeth.

Day 4

Society's Assumptions

(and why they are lies)

Take yesterday's most uncomfortable opinion.

Ask: What does society assume about this topic?

What is the correct opinion everyone performs?

Why does that assumption feel fake or incomplete to you?

Turn it into this structure:

"Everyone thinks ___, but actually………"

"Everyone thinks therapy means self-awareness, but actually it's customer service for your worst habits."

"Everyone thinks working from home means flexibility, but actually it means your boss lives in your laptop now."

Try three versions of the same idea.

Pick the one that makes you slightly nervous to say out loud.

Why this matters:

Comedy lives in the gap between official reality and actual reality.

You're not being contrarian.

You are being accurate in rooms that prefer comfort.

“Everyone thinks minimalism is tasteful, but it’s just financial security pretending to be a humble person.”

“So minimalist rich people don’t give each other gifts anymore. They already hid all that money somewhere it can’t be seen or taxed”.

Day 5

Exaggeration Day

(Push until it breaks}
Take yesterday's best

"Everyone thinks X, but actually Y" line.

Now push it too far. On purpose.

Make it absurd. Make it impossible.

Let it get ridiculous.

Don't fix it yet. Don't make it smart.

Just keep escalating until it breaks.

Examples:

Original:
"Self-care is so commercialized now."

Exaggerated:
"Self-care is so intense now I need a self-care day to recover from my self-care routine. I'm doing self-care for my self-care

routine. It’s called the self-care spiral.”

Write five exaggerated versions of your line.

Too far is fine. We're not keeping all of it. We're finding the energy of the joke by letting it run wild first.

Why this matters:
Exaggeration shows you the edges of your premise. Once you know how far is too far, you can pull back to exactly far enough. You can't edit what doesn't exist yet.

Watch for:

If your exaggeration just makes you sound angry rather than funny, you're punching when you should be pointing things out.

Day 6

The Out-Loud Test

(your phone is your audience)

Read your last 3 jokes out loud.

Record them on your phone.

Listen for:

Where you rush.
You don't trust the joke yet. Slow down.

Where you naturally pause.
That's your rhythm trying to emerge. Let it.

Where you smile — even micro-smiles.
That's where you find it funny. The audience will follow.

Clunky words.
Words that trip your tongue will trip theirs.

Simplify.
Rewrite only for sound. Not for intelligence. Not for poetry. For speakability.

Test:

If you can't say it smoothly three times in a row, it's not ready.

Why this matters:

Paper lies. It makes everything look smarter than it sounds. Your mouth knows better than your eyes.

Trust it.

Day 7

Your Default Comedy Mode

(stop imitating other comics)

People come to hear what only you can say.

In your own unique way.

With your own unique way of looking at situations.

Trust that.

Week Two:

Construction

(building jokes that do not collapse)

You already have a comedy setting. You've been using it your whole life without permission.

Finish these sentences honestly:

I tend to be funny when I'm ___ (emotion or situation)

My humour is more ___ than ___

My observations lean toward ___ (a specific quality)

Here are some common style pairings. Circle what fits. Cross out what doesn't:

- Dry > loud
- Observant > energetic
- Blunt > silly
- Deadpan > animated
- Absurdist > literal
- Conversational > theatrical
- Self-deprecating > boastful

• Smart-ass > goofy

Why this matters:

When you try to sound like a different kind of funny, your jokes get heavier and less true. When you work with your default setting, the comedy feels effortless—because it already is.

Circle your actual mode. Not the one you wish you had.

If you're trying to be the loud funny one, but you're actually the quiet sharp one, you will be bad at both.

Why this matters:

Comedy styles aren't better or worse. They're yours or not yours. Forcing someone else's rhythm is like walking in shoes two sizes wrong—you can do it, but why would you?

The trap:

Loud comedy gets more attention, so quiet comics think they're doing it wrong.

They're not. Different rooms need different voices.

Day 8

Everyday Moments

(Where comedy actually lives}

Forget big topics. Start with last Tuesday.

List 5 mundane situations from your real life:
Don't judge it. Just observe it.

Doctor's waiting room — observed, not joked yet.

Everyone lowers their voice like the room has a shared NDA. Reception conversations are quiet but extremely intense.

One person argues about paperwork; no one admits to hearing it. Phones come out, but nobody is actually enjoying their phone. The TV is on with subtitles no one is reading.

Magazines are from a year that feels emotionally unsafe. Your narc ex is on the cover and you are trying not to choke.

Every cough triggers silent judgment and mild panic.

When a name is called, everyone looks up, just in case.

People rehearse being calm while internally spiralling.

No one talks, but everyone is hyper-aware of everyone else.

The room runs on collective anxiety disguised as manners.

Picked: Doctor's waiting room.

What actually happens (not funny yet):

You walk in already a little defensive, as if your body might betray you at any moment. Everyone checks in at reception using their "polite sick voice," which is softer, slower, and weirdly apologetic. Names are mispronounced. Someone argues quietly about insurance like they're negotiating a hostage release. The rest of us pretend we are deeply invested in the floor tiles. Phones come out, we scroll mindlessly. Time stretches. The TV is on mute with subtitles that don't match. Magazines are from a past that clearly ended before the pandemic. Every cough causes a brief spike of paranoia.

When a nurse opens the door and calls a name, everyone looks up—just in case it's them—even though they know it's not. When it isn't, we all go back to pretending we weren't hoping.

Why are we pretending?

No one in that doctors' room acknowledges the tension, even though it's the loudest thing in the room. We all silently judge who looks "sicker," who doesn't belong, who's overreacting. The waiting room becomes a shared agreement to not talk about the obvious: we're anxious, bored, and slightly scared, together, but separately.

Why this matters:

Comedy isn't in the setting. It's in what you notice while everyone else is sleepwalking through it. Two people can sit in the same room and have completely different points of view, because one is waiting to be served and the other is watching.

Specific behaviour beats big ideas every time.

“Hospitals are stressful” isn’t comedy.

Watching people pretend they’re calm while gripping paperwork like it’s a flotation device in a drowning sea, is.

The joke isn’t the place—it’s the choreography.

The uniqueness of what you see.

Accuracy comes before cleverness.

When an audience recognizes the behaviour, they relax.

They trust you. Laughter follows recognition, not surprise. If they haven’t thought, “Oh god, yes, that’s exactly it,” the punchline won't land.

This is why observation is the real work.

Once you name what's actually happening—who's pretending, who's avoiding eye contact, who suddenly becomes fascinated by the floor—the punchlines start writing themselves.

Comedy isn't something you invent from thin air. It's something you uncover by paying attention longer than most people are willing to.

You're not exaggerating reality. You're clarifying it with your own unique world view. You're saying out loud the behaviour everyone else is silently clocking but politely ignoring.

That's why it lands. The audience isn't laughing because you surprised them—they are laughing because you caught them.

If you ever feel stuck, it's usually because you're trying to be funny too early. The urge to jump to a punchline is the enemy of good material. Stay with the behaviour longer.

Describe it more precisely. Strip out opinions. Strip out explanations. Let the facts sit there and hum.

Comedy rewards patience. The clearer you see what's happening, the less work the joke has to do. When the observation is accurate enough, the laugh isn't forced—it's inevitable.

Your job isn't to decorate reality.

Your job is to notice it.

Day 9

Expectation Vs Reality

(the engine of all comedy)

What you expected:

(what society promised; what logic suggests; what the fantasy version looks like)

What actually happens:

(the real; slightly broken; human version)

Why that gap annoys, confuses, or amuses you:

Every joke starts with an assumption.

What should happen.

What everyone quietly agrees is normal.
Then reality walks in late, wearing the wrong shoes.

Expectation is the story we tell ourselves.
Reality is what actually happens when

nobody's performing.

Comedy lives in the gap.

You expect the date to be charming and bring you flowers.
They start showing you photos of their protein powder collection and explaining macros like it's foreplay.

You expect the flight to board calmly.
But two strangers are already arguing about "who was standing near Gate 14 emotionally before it opened."

You expect the doctor to run on time.
The waiting room slowly turns into a support group for people googling their own symptoms.

You expect customer service to help you.
You get transferred to a flute instrumental version of your own problem.

You expect weddings to be romantic.
You spend three hours locating the correct WhatsApp group to figure out which entrance you have to enter from.

The bigger the expectation, the harder reality hits.

That impact is the laugh.

Your job today isn’t to exaggerate.

It is to notice the exact moment expectation collapses.

Exercise

Write one clear expectation in a situation.

Write exactly what actually happened.

Do not add a punchline yet.

Do not explain it.
Just sit in the contrast.
If the contrast is accurate, the joke 1S already there.
You're not inventing humour.

You're noticing friction.

You're documenting disappointment in real time.

Day 10

The Turn

(where the joke actually lands)

Add a turn to yesterday's observations.

Structure: "I thought ___, but then ___."

Or: "Everyone says ___, but actually ___."

Or: "The rule is ___, except ___."

Example:

"I thought minimalism would bring peace. But then I realized I'm just anxious in an empty room now. Same anxiety, less furniture."

Say it slowly. Pause right before the turn. That pause is sacred. It's the moment the audience's brain is still believing the setup. The turn hits harder when they are not ready.

Try 5 turns. Record them.

Listen for which turn surprises even you.

Why this matters:
The turn is the punchline's heartbeat. No turn = no joke, just observation. Master the turn and you can joke about anything.

Day 11

Trimming Fat

(comedy is subtraction)

Look at your last 5 jokes.
Cut ruthlessly:

Explaining (if your joke needs a footnote, it's not ready)
Justifying feelings (trust that your observation is enough)
Extra examples (one perfect detail beats three okay ones)

Hedge words: "kind of," "sort of," "maybe," "I think"

Before: "I kind of feel like self-care has sort of become this thing where we're almost making it into work, you know?"

After: "Self-care became work."

Then build from there if needed.

Test:

Read your joke.
Remove one word.
Does it still work?

Remove another.

Keep going until removing any word weakens it.

Why this matters:

Fat slows down the punch.

Every unnecessary word is a split-second the audience isn't laughing.

Respect their time.

Day 12

Self-Awareness Jokes

(put yourself in the mess)

Write 3 jokes where you are part of the problem you're describing.

Why this works:

Audiences trust comics who include themselves in the mess. Pointing at others = preaching. Pointing at yourself while pointing at others = comedy.

Examples:

"I judge people for being on their phones too much.

Then I realize I've been scrolling for 40 minutes

deciding which variety of scrolling to judge them for."

"I love when people are authentic. By which I

mean, when they're authentic in ways I approve of."

The formula:

Identify a behaviour you mock > admit you do it

too > add why you do it (that's the humanity)

Why this matters:

Self-awareness isn't self-deprecation. It's honesty with a wink. It says: "I see the game clearly, including my part in it."

Day 13

Tension

(the uncomfortable middle)

Comedy needs a little bit of "should I laugh at this?"
Add mild tension to your jokes:

Awkwardness (social rules breaking)

Contradiction (believing two opposite things)

Taboo (saying what we all think but don't say)

Discomfort (truth that stings a little)

Example:

"I love honesty. But only when it flatters me. When it doesn't, I love nuance."

Write 3 jokes with tension.

If they make you slightly uncomfortable, you're on track.

Why this matters:

Tension is the difference between an observation and a joke. No tension = no release.

No release = no laugh.

Warning:

Tension without empathy is just cruelty. Make sure you're laughing with the human condition, not at any specific humans.

Day 14

Silence Practice

(the pause is half the joke)

Say your best joke from this week.
Insert a 2-second pause before the punchline.
Physically count: one-tick tick one, two-tick tick two...

Let the audience walk into the joke themselves.

Their brain is doing setup math.

Don't interrupt it.

Example:

"I started meditating for inner peace." [PAUSE]

"Now I'm just aware of my anxiety in real time.

I'm now officially mindfully & consciously stressed."

Record yourself doing this 5 times.

Notice: the pause feels eternal to you. To the audience, it's perfect.

Why this matters:

Silence is active.

It's not dead air—it's the joke loading.

Rushing the punchline is like explaining the magic trick before it's done.

Week Three:

Assembly

(Building a set that doesn't feel like homework}

Day 15

The Mini Set

(your first ninety seconds)

Assemble your first mini-set.

Structure:

Opening line (relatable, not a joke yet—just connection)

Joke 1 (your strongest, clearest premise)

Joke 2 (builds on similar theme or pivots smoothly)

Closing line (callback or personal button)

Example:

" I thought I needed relaxation and rejuvenation, so I went to a luxury wellness resort. [opener]

Instead of relaxing me, they helped me discover problems I didn't even know I had. Now I'm still trying to figure out...
did I actually have a breakthrough...

or did I just hallucinate new insecurities in eucalyptus steam? [joke 1]

I used to worry so much. Which is why I went to the wellness sort in the first place.
Just simple, basic, middle-class worry.
Now I've been diagnosed with *Chronic Over-Processing Emotional Feedback Loop Disorder.*
Same hell. Fancier brochure. And from middle class I've now become poor [joke 2]

"My therapist is very proud of my progress.
My anxiety now has a LinkedIn profile.
It's networking with other disorders...
and honestly, it's doing better than me."
[closer]

Read them in order. Out loud. Standing.

Notice flow, not perfection. Does one joke earn the next?

Why this matters:

Three connected jokes prove you have a point of view, not just random observations. This is where you stop being clever and start being a comic.

Day 16

What Bombs on Paper

(the clever trap)

Underline jokes that feel clever but cold.

They usually:

Show intelligence more than emotion.
Use wordplay that requires a rewind.
Hide your actual feelings behind technique.
Sound like tweets, not stories.

Example of clever but cold:
"Minimalism is the aesthetic of having already bought everything twice."

It's smart. It's true. It's... lifeless.

Rewrite with feeling:
"I tried minimalism. Turns out I'm not enlightened, I just can't afford more shit. My spirituality is on a budget."

Rewrite 3 "clever" jokes with more feeling, less flex.

Why this matters:

Clever gets respect. Feeling gets laughs.

You want laughs.

Day 17

Audience Imagination

(clarity vs dumbing down)

Imagine three people:

Your funniest friend (gets all your references)
A stranger at a bus stop (no context about you)
Your harshest critic (looking for reasons to dismiss you)

Say the same joke to all three. In your head.

Adjust for:
Friend: You can be more cryptic, they'll follow.

Stranger: Do they have enough context?

Critic: Are you clear enough they can't pretend to miss the point?

The goal: Clarity that doesn't insult intelligence.

Why this matters:
You're not dumbing down. You're removing barriers between your brain and theirs.

Big difference.

Day 18

Confidence Without Loudness

(delivery is belief)

Rewrite one joke as if you:

Don't need approval.

Aren't apologizing (no "I mean" or "kind of")

Are amused first (you're not convincing them it's funny—you already know)

Before:

"So I guess I'm kind of realizing that self-care is sort of like... work now? I don't know, maybe that's just me."

After:

"Self-care became work. I have a productivity app for my bubble baths."

Notice the shift:

Belief sounds like simplicity. Doubt sounds like clauses.

Why this matters:

Delivery isn't volume. It's certainty. You're not asking if it's funny. You're informing them that it is.

Day 19

Your First 3 Minutes

(The actual set}

Build a 3-minute set:

Opening (15 seconds): Relatable, warm, human.

Chunk 1 (60 seconds): Your strongest premise + 2- 3 supporting jokes.

Chunk 2 (60 seconds): Different angle, same voice.

Closer (15 seconds): Callback or personal truth.

Example structure:

"I've been working on myself. That's what we call it now when we're a mess with a plan..."

[3-4 jokes about self-improvement culture]

[Pivot to relationships/work/something connected]

[End with a button that ties back]

This is enough. Don't overbuild.

More material = more places to die.

Why this matters:
Three tight minutes beats ten shaggy minutes every time. Quality scales.

Quantity just reveals where you should have stopped.

Day 20

Record Your Set

(The moment of truth}

Record yourself performing the 3 minutes. Standing up. No notes. Like it's real.

Watch it once. Just once.

Note (without spiralling):

What landed (you'll feel it)

What dragged (you'll feel that too)

Where you lost confidence (your voice changes)

What you'd cut immediately

Do not watch it 47 times looking for proof you're terrible.

You're not. You're learning.

Why this matters:

Seeing yourself perform is horrifying and

necessary. It's the only way to know what you think you're doing vs what you're actually doing.

Day 21

Your Comedy Manifesto

(the compass you ll need later)

Finish these sentences. Seriously.

Write them down.

Comedy, for me, is ___

I refuse to joke about ___

I want audiences to feel ___

Example:

Comedy, for me, is clarity with a laugh track. I refuse to joke about things I haven't experienced or punch down for convenience. I want audiences to feel less alone in their weirdness.

Why this matters:

Trends will try to hijack your voice.

Algorithms will pressure you to be someone else. This manifesto is your tether. When you're confused about what joke to make, come back here.

The Final Truth

(that no one wants to hear)

You don't "become" funny.

You stop censoring the part of you that already is.

Comedy isn't:

Confidence first > jokes later

It's:

Jokes first > confidence follows.

Volume follows proof.

Every comedian you admire spent years being unfunny in rooms full of strangers. They just didn't let that stop them. Neither should you.

One Last Thing

You're not practicing comedy.

You're building a thinking style.

A way of moving through the world that notices gaps, contradictions, and absurdities—then names them before they name you.

That skill transfers.

To writing. To conversation. To not taking yourself so seriously you forget how to breathe.

The jokes are just proof you're paying attention.

Now go write something bad.

On purpose.

With JOY.

PS: If you finish this and still think you're not funny, you're not unfunny. You are just scared. There's a difference.

PPS: Every great comedian is just a terrified person who decided to talk anyway.

PPPS: You're that person. Talk.

PPPPS: Okay I'll stop now.

pssst: Now go have fun with this.

With Love and laughs,

That Funny Gal

If you enjoyed this book, please consider leaving a review.

Your feedback helps other readers discover it.

Explore more titles by The Crackajack Company.

9 788169 067874